W9-AHJ-807

EASY
597.95

C 51354

Martin, Louise
  Chameleons.

DATE DUE

MAR 1 2 2003	JAN 9 0 2008
MAR 1 7 2003	MAR 3 1 2008
OCT 2 8 2005	OCT 2 9 2017
FEB 0 5 2007	NOV 1 9 2017
JAN 0 2 2008	

DEMCO 128-5046

OCT 3 0 2001
DEC 2 0 2001

BEECHER ROAD SCHOOL LIBRARY
WOODBRIDGE, CT 06525

OCT 1 5 2002

JAN 2 1 2003

FEB 2 4 2003   MAR 2 0 2008

OCT 0 7 2008

EASY
597.95   BEECHER ROAD
         SCHOOL LIBARARY
         Chameleons.

51354

CHAMELEONS

THE REPTILE DISCOVERY LIBRARY

Louise Martin

Rourke Enterprises, Inc.
Vero Beach, Florida 32964

© 1989 Rourke Enterprises, Inc.

All rights reserved. No part of this book
may be reproduced or utilized in any form
or by any means, electronic or mechanical
including photocopying, recording or by any
information storage and retrieval system
without permission in writing from the
publisher.

Library of Congress Cataloging-in-Publication Data

Martin, Louise, 1955-
  Chameleons.

  (The Reptile discovery library)
  Includes index.
  Summary: An introduction to the physical
characteristics, habits, and natural
environments of various species of
lizards that are able to change their
skin color to blend in with their
surroundings.
    1. Chameleons—Juvenile literature. [1. Chameleons]
I. Title.
II. Series: Martin, Louise, 1955-
Reptile discovery library.
QL666.L23M37   1989   597.95   88-29730
ISBN 0-86592-576-3

TABLE OF CONTENTS

CHAMELEONS

Chameleons are small, lizard-like creatures. They are famous for being able to change their skin color to blend in with their surroundings. There are 85 **species** of chameleons. They vary greatly in size. Most are between eight and twelve inches long. The giant chameleon *(Chamaeleo onstaleti)* can grow up to two feet long. At one and one-half inches, the tiny dwarf chameleon *(Brookesia minima)* may be the world's smallest **reptile**.

This chameleon matches the bright green of the plants around it

HOW THEY LOOK

Chameleons can change their skin color from shades of brown and gray to green, yellow, and even blue. They do not always change color just for **camouflage**, or to keep from being seen. If a chameleon is angry or frightened, it will probably become darker. Temperature and light also affect chameleons' skin color. Some chameleons, like this Jackson's chameleon *(Chamaeleo Jacksoni)*, have sharp horns.

Chameleons can adopt stripes and even spots to help their camouflage

WHERE THEY LIVE

Common chameleons *(Chamaeleo chameleon)* live in many parts of North Africa and in southern Spain. All kinds of chameleons are common in Africa, south of the Sahara Desert. About half of the 85 species of chameleons can be found on the island of Madagascar off the east coast of Africa. Chameleons spend most of their lives in trees, leaving them only to build nests at ground level.

Chameleons are usually seen in trees

WHAT THEY EAT

Chameleons are **carnivorous**, or meat-eating. Some of the larger species of chameleons eat small **mammals**. Mellor's chameleon *(Chamaeleo Melleri)*, which grows to fourteen inches, eats small birds. Most chameleons, though, live on a diet of insects. Chameleons move so slowly and quietly that their **prey** usually does not see them coming. Gently, they move into position to strike.

Chameleons sometimes eat grasshoppers

A pair of chameleons in a threatening pose

When chameleons outgrow their skins they shed them

HOW THEY EAT

Chameleons' sticky tongues are half as long as their bodies. These are attached to their mouths by a strong bone. The tongues have hollow tips. They close around the prey so that it has no means of escape. Chameleons keep their tongues curled up in their mouths until they are ready to attack. The tongues lash out like lightning. They never miss a target.

A Jackson's chameleon catches a fly with its long, sticky tongue

THEIR SENSES

Chameleons' eyes are covered with skin. They see through a tiny hole in the middle. Chameleons can look backward and forward at the same time. They can focus one eye on one object and the other on something in the opposite direction. This means a chameleon can look at its prey and at the same time watch for **predators** that might try to make dinner out of the chameleon!

This chameleon is looking in two different directions

LIVING IN THE TREES

Chameleons' feet and tails are specially designed for living in trees. Their strong, **prehensile** tails curl easily around branches and twigs. Chameleons can hang upside down by their tails. Each of the chameleons' four feet has five toes. The toes are positioned two opposite three, giving chameleons a firm grip. Sharp little claws give extra grip when it is needed.

Chameleons use their tails and toes to firmly grasp the branches

BABY CHAMELEONS

Most chameleons lay eggs in a nest in the ground. In the rain forests, the eggs are laid in soft, rotting leaf litter. Female chameleons usually lay their eggs in batches of thirty to forty. They cover them up and leave them. Three months later the eggs crack open, and the baby chameleons are hatched. Dwarf chameleons bear live young, the eggs hatching as they are laid.

Female chameleons dig nests in the ground where they lay their eggs

THEIR DEFENSES

Chameleons may fight other chameleons if their living space becomes too crowded. Sometimes they bite and even kill each other. Normally, a threat display is enough to make one chameleon give in to another. The fighting chameleons puff up their bodies and throat pouches and arch their backs, rocking to and fro with a hiss. Often, they rise up onto their back legs to frighten each other.

GLOSSARY

camouflage (KAM uh flazh) — a way of hiding by blending in with the surroundings

carnivorous (car NIV uh rus) — meat-eating

mammals (MAM uls) — animals that give birth to live young and feed them with mother's milk

predators (PRE duh turz) — animals that hunt other animals for food

prehensile (pre HENS ile) — a tail or limb able to firmly grasp and cling to a branch

prey (PRAY) — an animal hunted by another for food

reptile (REP tile) — a cold-blooded, usually scaly-skinned animal

species (SPEE seez) — a scientific term meaning kind or type

INDEX